Earl's Story

A True Story
By Janet Hutchinson

I am a young egret from Chile. One day, I lost my way.

I landed on a sailboat named "Dulcinea."

I was cold and frightened.

But there were friendly people on board.

They gave me squid to eat.

I drank water from a green bucket.

I washed my feet every day.

On the boat there were two big wheels ...

lots of ropes ...

and some in a tangle!

I went inside the cabin.

I looked at the world map. Where were we going?

The people took me outside again.

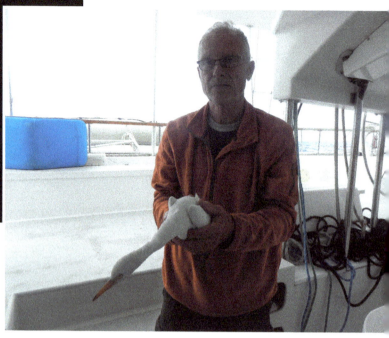

I enjoyed exercising.

I also enjoyed resting.

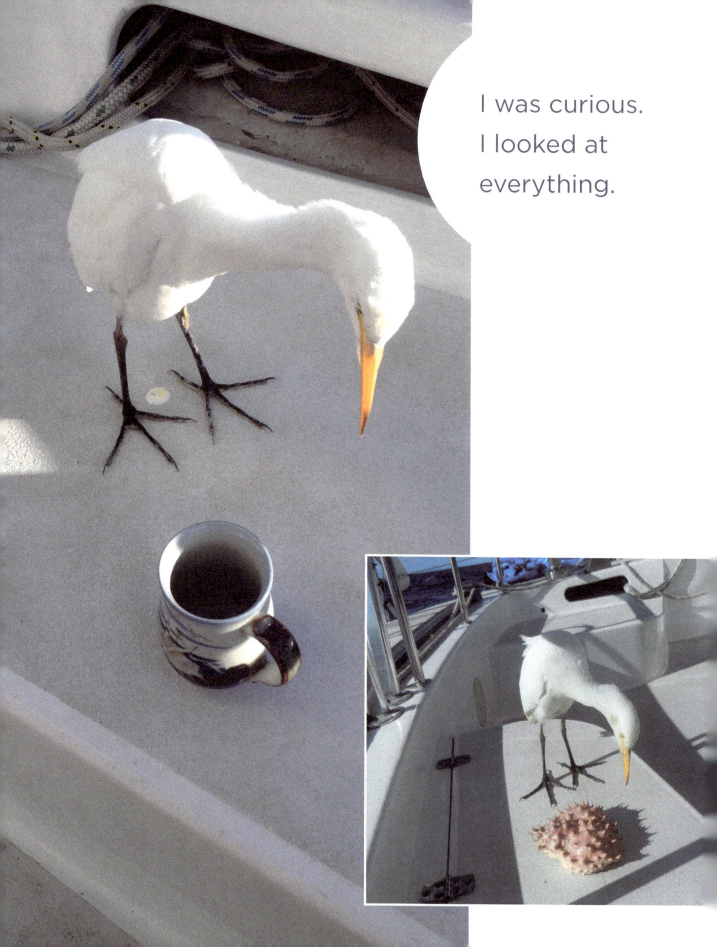

I was curious. I looked at everything.

Orange peel looked tasty.

I loved eating squid heads.

Big and small fish landed on the boat each night.

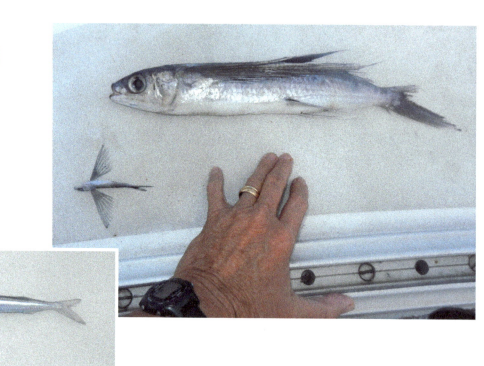

The people fed them to me.

I wanted to learn how to read.

I liked to be near people.

I helped clean the boat.

I watched the world through the windows.

Sometimes, big boats went by.

I stood around.

But I kept returning to the boat.

        I stayed on the boat for three weeks.

Then, one day, I left the
boat in French Polynesia.
Goodbye, Dulcinea.

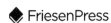 FriesenPress

Suite 300 - 990 Fort St
Victoria, BC, V8V 3K2
Canada

www.friesenpress.com

Copyright © 2018 by Janet Hutchinson
First Edition — 2018

www.techco.ab.ca/dulcinea

All rights reserved.

No part of this publication may be reproduced in any form, or by any means, electronic or mechanical, including photocopying, recording, or any information browsing, storage, or retrieval system, without permission in writing from FriesenPress.

ISBN
978-1-5255-2003-7 (Hardcover)
978-1-5255-2004-4 (Paperback)
978-1-5255-2005-1 (eBook)

1. JUVENILE NONFICTION, ANIMALS, BIRDS

Distributed to the trade by The Ingram Book Company

CPSIA information can be obtained
at www.ICGtesting.com
Printed in the USA
LVHW01*0927160418
573598LV00004B/10/P